GROSS
GOODIES

Tina Vilicich-Solomon

Illustrated by Neal Yamamoto

Lowell House
Juvenile
Los Angeles

CONTEMPORARY BOOKS
Chicago

For Dan, thanks for teaching me that anything gross
can be good for a laugh . . . I love you!
—T. V. S.

Publisher: Jack Artenstein
Associate Publisher, Juvenile Division: Elizabeth Amos
Director of Publishing Services: Rena Copperman
Managing Editor, Juvenile Division: Lindsey Hay
Editor in Chief, Nonfiction Juvenile: Amy Downing
Art Director: Lisa Theresa Lenthall
Cover illustration: Su-Zan

Library of Congress Catalog Card Number is available.

ISBN: 1-56565-550-8

Lowell House books can be purchased at special discounts when ordered in bulk for premiums and special sales. Contact Department JH at the following address:

Lowell House Juvenile
2029 Century Park East, Suite 3290
Los Angeles, CA 90067

Manufactured in the United States of America
10 9 8 7 6 5 4 3 2 1

Contents

Introduction

When you peel off a scab-filled bandage, does your mouth water with anticipation? Do you long to nibble on that earwax-encrusted cotton swab? Then get set to satisfy that secretly sick and strange desire for bad taste! *Gross Goodies* is the consummate cookbook for culinary creeps with a hankering for something sickening and sweet. Whether you're rolling out a quick batch of Crusty Booger Balls or whipping up Toilet Paper Wads, all the repugnant recipes in this book are designed to satisfy the crudest of cooks and the truly grotesque gourmand!

RULES TO REMEMBER

1 Always go over the recipe with an adult before you begin any cooking project. Make sure that person has enough time to help you complete the recipe.

2 Read through your recipe before you begin to make sure you've got all the ingredients and tools you'll require.

3 Clean up as you go. Wipe down counters, put dirty dishes in the sink, and rinse out bowls as you finish with them. That way, cleaning up is quick, and you'll be allowed back into the kitchen to gross out future guests.

4 Be sure all your ingredients are fresh. Check expiration dates on all milk and dairy products.

5 Re-read the recipe a few times as you're cooking to be sure you don't forget any steps. Also, if you're a novice gourmet, keep distractions, such as TV and friends, out of the kitchen until you're finished. You'll be able to concentrate on grossing everyone out with a recipe that's a success instead of stressing yourself out with one that was goofed!

KITCHEN SAFETY

1 When a recipe calls for adult supervision, make sure the adult is right beside you—in the next room doesn't count.

2 Get yourself ready: Be sure to wash your hands with warm water and soap before you begin handling food. Dry them thoroughly so they're not slippery. If you've got long hair, tie it back to prevent it from falling into food or getting caught in the burner flame or mixer's beater. Protect your clothing —tie on an apron.

3 Use pot holders whenever you hold pan handles, open or close the oven, and especially when putting items into and taking them out of the oven.

4 When cooking on the stovetop, always turn handles in toward the side of the stove. Handles hanging out over the edge can lead to dangerous spills or burns.

5 When you're finished using a sharp knife, stop a moment to rinse it off and place it somewhere safe. Never drop a sharp knife into sudsy water—you may reach in and forget it's there!

6 Always be sure burners and oven are turned off when not in use. Appliances you've used, such as blenders and mixers, should be put safely back where they belong.

7 When using knives, always cut down, carefully, onto a cutting board and NEVER cut in toward the palm of your hand.

8 Steam can burn your skin as badly as boiling water, so use extra caution when draining foods cooked in hot liquid.

9 When using electrical appliances, such as a blender or mixer, make sure your hands are completely dry. Never remove an appliance from an outlet by pulling on the cord.

10 Make sure the kitchen has a working fire extinguisher. If you don't know how to use it, ask an adult to show you.

UTENSILS EVERY BAKER
SHOULD HAVE

baking sheet - A flat pan with no sides, designed specifically for even heating of items such as cookies.

colander - A perforated bowl used for washing and draining food.

cutting board - A plastic mat or wooden block designed to protect countertops from damage while chopping or cutting.

dry-measuring cups - Often made of plastic, these measuring cups come in stacked sizes ranging from $\frac{1}{8}$ cup to 2 cups. They are designed so that ingredients can be scooped, then leveled off with a rubber spatula or butter knife.

electric mixer - An electric appliance, often hand-held, that's designed to quickly mix ingredients. Note: If you don't have one, most recipes can be mixed by hand by using either a wooden spoon, whisk, or heavy-duty rubber spatula.

mixing bowls - You'll need various-sized mixing bowls, depending on the individual recipe. Bowls should be deep enough for electric beaters to fit in without splattering ingredients over the sides.

pastry bag - Pastry bags can be purchased in most supermarket baking sections or craft supply stores. A heavy-duty plastic bag, snipped at one corner, is a fine substitute and can be filled with frosting or whipped cream.

rubber spatula - A flat rubber tool with a long handle and a flexible tip, used for scraping bowls and evenly spreading ingredients, such as frosting.

standard measuring cup - This measuring cup is usually made of clear plastic or glass and designed with a pour spout for pouring liquid measurements.

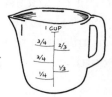

strainer - A bowl-shaped utensil with a handle and fine-mesh interior used for filtering out large pieces of food items from liquid or semi-liquid ingredients.

utility knife - A 6- to 8-inch knife with a smooth, sharp blade.

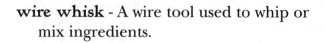

wire whisk - A wire tool used to whip or mix ingredients.

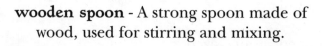

wooden spoon - A strong spoon made of wood, used for stirring and mixing.

GLOSSARY OF BAKING TERMS

baste - To drip from the baking pan back onto food in order to maintain its moistness and flavor.

boil - To heat a liquid to the point where air bubbles form at the bottom of pan.

dash - A very slight addition of an ingredient, such as one sprinkle or ⅛ teaspoon half filled.

fold - A gentle way to combine light ingredients, such as whipped cream, with heavier ingredients, such as fruit, with minimal mixing.

invert - To flip over and empty a pan or tray onto another surface, such as a cake plate or cutting board.

line - To cover the interior of a baking sheet, pan, or bowl with removable protection, such as aluminum foil (which can be put in the oven), waxed paper, and plastic wrap.

mix - To evenly blend ingredients by either stirring or beating.

peel - The outer skin of fruit or the action of removing the outer skin from fruit.

pith - The soft white part of peelings from citrus fruits (lemons, limes, and oranges) that is between the colorful exterior (zest) and the edible portion of the fruit.

puree - To finely grind ingredients into a semi-liquid form.

set - When ingredients, such as gelatin, are firm and completely congealed.

turn out - To empty contents of a pan or tray onto a work surface or serving platter (see **invert**).

zest - The colorful outermost portion of citrus fruits.

MEASURING TIPS

When measuring . . .

liquids - Use a clear measuring cup with a pour spout. Bend down to check the correct amount at eye level.

dry ingredients - Flour, granulated sugar, spices, and other dry items are measured by using a dry-measuring cup or spoon. After filling appropriate cup or spoon, accurate measuring is achieved by leveling off ingredient with a spatula.

chopped ingredients - Chopped items, such as nuts, should be chopped first then placed into a dry-measuring cup and packed lightly.

brown sugar - Pack brown sugar lightly into a dry-measuring cup by using the palm of your clean hand, the bottom of a large spoon, or a rubber spatula.

margarine or butter - Paper wrappers have measurement indications on one side. With an adult's help, simply cut along the appropriate line with your butter knife. Be sure butter or margarine is not yet softened. If you are using margarine from a tub, pack it firmly into a dry-measuring cup. Pat it down with a rubber spatula to remove any air pockets.

MEASUREMENTS
EVERY GROSS GOURMET SHOULD KNOW

3 teaspoons = 1 tablespoon	2 cups = 1 pint
4 tablespoons = ¼ cup	4 cups = 1 quart
8 tablespoons = ½ cup	2 quarts = ½ gallon
16 tablespoons = 1 cup	4 quarts = 1 gallon
16 ounces = 1 pound	

8 tablespoons or ½ cup butter = 1 stick butter

4 sticks or 2 cups butter = 1 pound butter

INFECTED CONFECTIONS & COAGULATED CANDIES

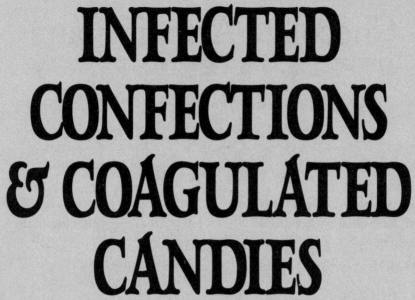

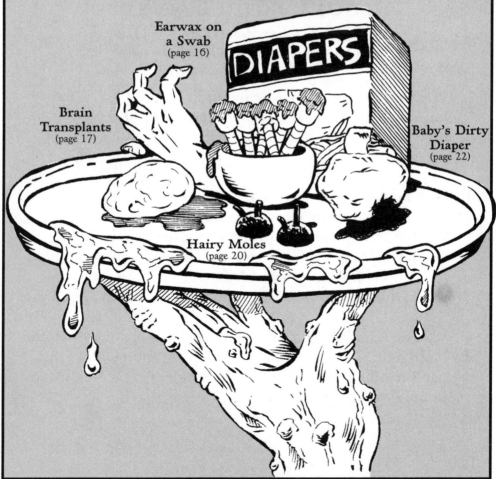

Earwax on
a Swab
(page 16)

Brain
Transplants
(page 17)

Baby's Dirty
Diaper
(page 22)

Hairy Moles
(page 20)

DIAPERS

Chocolate Armpit Hairs

There's nothing tastier than a batch of armpit hairs,
freshly shaved from a sweaty pit.

INGREDIENTS

3 large shredded wheat bundles, such as Nabisco Shredded Wheat ®

3 tablespoons honey

1 tablespoon light brown sugar

1 6-ounce bag milk-chocolate chips

2 tablespoons butter

TOOLS YOU'LL NEED

• medium-sized, heavy saucepan • pot holder
• rubber spatula • waxed paper • fork

1 Break up the shredded wheat bundles into single long strands, so that they have the appearance of armpit hairs. Set aside.

2 With an adult's help, place the honey, brown sugar, chocolate chips, and butter in a medium-sized heavy saucepan and heat over a low flame to melt. Use a pot holder to hold the pan's handle as you gently stir the chocolate mixture with a rubber spatula. Mixture should be smooth and glossy.

3 With an adult's help, remove the saucepan from burner and place it on a heat-safe work surface. Continue to hold the pan's handle steady with your pot holder as you gently fold in the shredded wheat.

4 When the shredded wheat is completely coated, scoop it onto the waxed paper in nine equal portions. Use a fork to gently rake hairs into one direction.

5 To set Chocolate Armpit Hairs, place them in the refrigerator for about thirty minutes. If there are any hairy bundles left over, keep them stored in the refrigerator.

Serves: 9 hairy hooligans

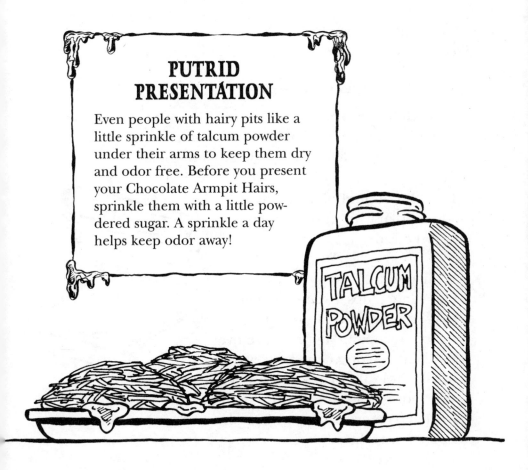

PUTRID PRESENTATION

Even people with hairy pits like a little sprinkle of talcum powder under their arms to keep them dry and odor free. Before you present your Chocolate Armpit Hairs, sprinkle them with a little powdered sugar. A sprinkle a day helps keep odor away!

Diarrhea Delights

Serve these painful confections to all the neighborhood kids.
Those little squirts will come a runnin'!

INGREDIENTS

3 6-ounce packages semi-sweet chocolate chips

1 14-ounce can sweetened condensed milk

dash of salt (⅛ teaspoon half filled)

2 teaspoons vanilla extract

1½ cups chopped, dried mixed fruit (the type used for fruit cakes)

TOOLS YOU'LL NEED

• 9-inch square pan • waxed paper • large heavy saucepan
• wire whisk • pot holder • wooden spoon • spatula
• cutting board • large cutting knife

1 Line the bottom of a 9-inch square pan with waxed paper and set aside.

2 With an adult's help, pour chocolate chips, sweetened condensed milk, and salt into large heavy saucepan. Melt mixture over low heat, stirring constantly with a whisk. Hold the pan's handle steady with your pot holder as you stir. When mixture is completely melted, remove saucepan from heat. Place pan on a heat-safe work surface.

3 Pour in vanilla and dried mixed fruit. Continue to hold the pan's handle with the pot holder and use a wooden spoon to thoroughly blend fruit into chocolate mixture.

4 With an adult's help, pour chocolate mixture into lined pan and spread it evenly with your rubber spatula. Place pan in the refrigerator and chill for at least two hours.

5 When thoroughly chilled, invert chocolate mixture onto cutting board. With an adult's help, use a large cutting knife to cut into 1-inch squares.

6 Create loads of uniquely shaped diarrhea dumps by rolling each square between the palms of your clean, dry hands. Make some flat, round disks, some short, thick poops, and some long, skinny ones!

Makes: About 2 pounds dandy doo-doo

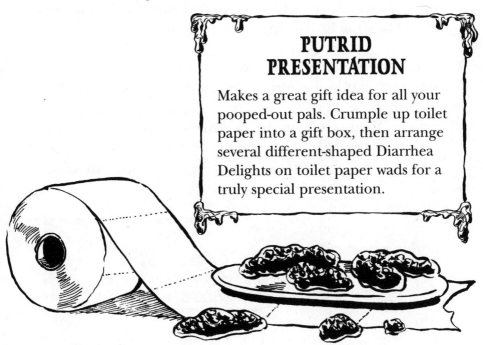

PUTRID PRESENTATION

Makes a great gift idea for all your pooped-out pals. Crumple up toilet paper into a gift box, then arrange several different-shaped Diarrhea Delights on toilet paper wads for a truly special presentation.

Earwax on a Swab

It's a dirty shame more people don't know how yummy sweet, chewy earwax can be.

INGREDIENTS

24 mini marshmallows   6 ounces butterscotch chips

TOOLS YOU'LL NEED

• scissors • approximately 12 solid-colored straight drinking straws
• small microwave-safe bowl • pot holder
• waxed paper • toothpick

1 Snip straws into 2½-inch lengths. You should have twenty-four 2½-inch straws. To form cotton swabs, firmly press a mini marshmallow onto the end of each straw piece.

2 Place butterscotch chips into microwave-safe bowl and microwave at low power or defrost setting for about thirty seconds. Use a pot holder and ask an adult to help you remove the bowl from the microwave. Stir the butterscotch with a toothpick and return it to the microwave. Repeat this process until the butterscotch looks completely melted.

3 Dip the very tip of each cotton swab into the melted earwax and place sideways on waxed paper to harden.

Serves: 6 earwax eaters

Brain Transplants

These are the perfect treats to serve your "brainless" friends.

INGREDIENTS

3½ cups flaked coconut

2 cups confectioners' sugar

¼ cup butter, softened

¼ cup light cream

1 teaspoon almond extract

¾ cup grenadine syrup

TOOLS YOU'LL NEED

• large mixing bowl • rubber spatula
• baking sheet • waxed paper • rounded tablespoon

1 In a large bowl, combine all the ingredients except for the grenadine syrup. Mix well using a rubber spatula.

2 Line cookie sheet with waxed paper. Use a rounded tablespoon to scoop out and form brain shapes. Drop mixture by spoonfuls onto lined cookie sheet. Each brain should be similar in shape to a hard-boiled egg cut in half lengthwise.

3 Place cookie sheet in the refrigerator to chill for at least an hour. Use your hands to reshape any brains that need it.

4 Just before serving, pour about 3 tablespoons grenadine syrup on each plate to create the blood necessary for brains to stay alive during transplantation (and consumption!). Place two brains on each plate. Store extras in the refrigerator.

Serves: 1 dozen mad scientists

17

Crusty Booger Balls

Everyone will adore this delightful texture combination of both crunch and chew—hand-picked especially by you!

INGREDIENTS

1 14-ounce can sweetened condensed milk

5⅓ cups flaked coconut (about 14 ounces)

1 large 8-ounce package lime-flavored gelatin

1 cup ground, blanched almonds

1 teaspoon almond extract

TOOLS YOU'LL NEED

• large mixing bowl • large mixing spoon or rubber spatula • plastic wrap • waxed paper • baking sheet

1 In a large bowl, combine sweetened condensed milk, coconut, ⅓ cup of the unprepared gelatin, almonds, and almond extract. Mix well with a large mixing spoon or rubber spatula.

2 Cover bowl with plastic wrap and chill for about an hour or until mixture is firm enough to mold in your hands. Scoop by ½ teaspoonfuls and shape into various-sized booger balls. Place them on a baking sheet, lined with a sheet of waxed paper. Make sure they are all slightly different, just as each and every booger is unique and special.

3 Place a second sheet of waxed paper on your work surface and pour remaining unprepared lime gelatin on the center of the waxed paper. Roll each ball in

gelatin to coat well and create a thin outer layer. Then place back on the baking sheet.

4 Return boogers to the refrigerator for an hour before serving, and store any extras in the refrigerator.

Makes: About 5 dozen just-picked treats

PUTRID PRESENTATION

Hide one of the boogers in your hand and pretend you're pulling it out of your nose. Then roll it between your fingers and plop it on a serving plate.

SNORT!

Hairy Moles

Holy moley, bakers! This recipe's quicker to make than a trip to the dermatologist's office!

INGREDIENTS

½ cup margarine or butter

1 cup unsweetened cocoa

1 14-ounce can sweetened condensed milk

1 teaspoon vanilla extract

4 strands black shoelace licorice

TOOLS YOU'LL NEED

- medium-sized, heavy saucepan with lid • wooden spoon
- pot holder • kitchen scissors • shallow bowl
- waxed paper • baking sheet

1 With an adult's help, place margarine or butter in a medium-sized heavy saucepan on low heat. When butter has melted, add ¾ cup of the unsweetened cocoa and all the sweetened condensed milk. Mix well with a wooden spoon until smooth and thoroughly blended. Use a pot holder to hold the handle steady. With an adult's help, continue to cook and stir over medium heat until thickened and smooth, about five minutes.

2 With an adult's help, use a pot holder to remove mole mixture from heat and place it on a heat-safe surface. Stir in vanilla extract. Cover saucepan with lid and chill in the refrigerator for at least three hours or until firm.

3 While you're waiting, prepare the mole whiskers by snipping the licorice into ½-inch lengths. Set aside. Place remaining unsweetened cocoa in a shallow bowl and set aside. Lay out a 2-foot sheet of waxed paper on a baking sheet and set aside on your work surface.

4 Once mixture is firm, scoop a rounded teaspoonful into your clean, dry hands and shape moles into 1¼-inch round balls. Roll each mole in reserved cocoa. Insert one or two whiskers of different lengths into each mole and place moles on waxed paper.

5 When complete, place the entire baking sheet in the refrigerator for at least an hour to completely chill and firm these hairy moles.

Makes: About 4 dozen bite-sized hairy growths

PUTRID PRESENTATION

Tear out full-page head shots of models from old beauty magazines and place them on the table as dessert "plates." Then before calling your guests to the table, instantly transform those beautiful women into scary hags by placing your Hairy Moles on their chins or noses!

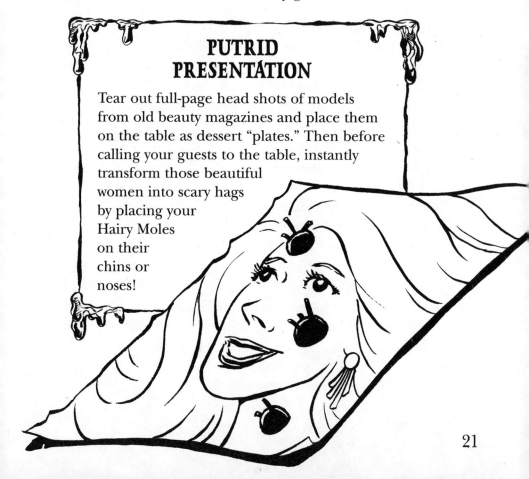

Baby's Dirty Diapers

*Quick and easy, you can push these
little stinkers out in no time!*

INGREDIENTS

6 caramel squares   24 large marshmallows

TOOLS YOU'LL NEED
• kitchen scissors • toaster oven
• toaster oven tray or heavy-duty aluminum foil
• pot holder

1 Unwrap caramel squares and, with an adult's help, cut them in four equal parts with your kitchen scissors. Set aside. Next, snip marshmallows partway down the center, lengthwise (see illustration). To create a diaper, the marshmallow needs to stay in one piece, so make sure you don't cut all the way through.

2 Snip two triangle-shaped wedges off the marshmallow's bottom to create leg openings.Insert one piece of caramel into the cut center of each sliced marshmallow.

3 With your clean hands, pinch the sides of the marshmallow back together around the caramel piece. Gently pinch and pull the sides of the marshmallow to form your diaper.

4 Arrange the diapers on the toaster oven tray or a square of heavy-duty foil about 2 inches apart. Toast on a "light toast" setting for about thirty seconds or until marshmallows begin to bubble. The diapers will melt and lose shape quickly, so be careful not to overcook. With an adult's help, use a pot holder to remove diapers from oven and cool slightly. Dirty diapers taste best when they're fresh and warm.

Makes: 24 party poopers

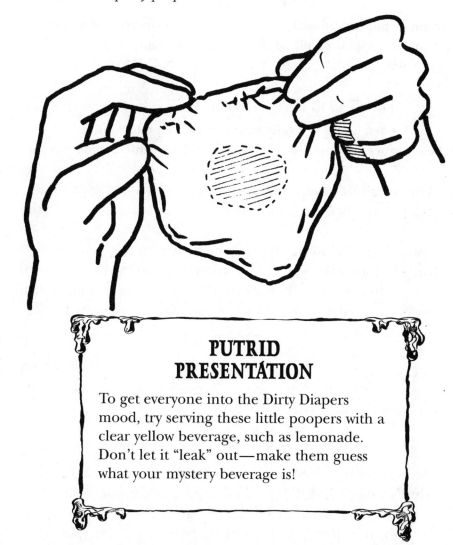

PUTRID PRESENTATION

To get everyone into the Dirty Diapers mood, try serving these little poopers with a clear yellow beverage, such as lemonade. Don't let it "leak" out—make them guess what your mystery beverage is!

Candied Skin Grafts

*These sticky patches of peeled-off skin look frightful,
but they taste "skin"fully good.*

INGREDIENTS

1 cup water, plus additional water
   for simmering grapefruit peels
5 grapefruits

1 ½ teaspoons ground ginger
2 ½ cups granulated sugar

TOOLS YOU'LL NEED

• tea kettle • utility knife • kitchen tablespoon
• heavy saucepan with lid • colander • heavy-duty aluminum foil

1 With an adult's help, place some water in a tea kettle and
bring it to a boil over high heat.

2 Also with an adult's help, use the utility knife to cut grapefruits in half, crosswise. Next, use the kitchen tablespoon to
scoop out the fruit, then store it for use later. Cut grapefruit
peels into strips, ¼- to ½-inch wide, with your utility knife.

3 Place grapefruit peel strips in a heavy saucepan. With an
adult's help, carefully pour enough boiling water over the
peels to cover them in 1 inch of water. Simmer them for
five minutes. Remove from heat. To drain the strips, place a

colander in the sink and have an adult empty the strips into the colander. Repeat this step four more times with the same peels using fresh boiling water each time. Drain the strips well after each simmering. (This will remove the bitter oils from the peel.) After final draining, set peels aside in colander.

4 In the same heavy saucepan, combine ginger, 1 cup water, and 2 cups of the sugar. With an adult's help, simmer over medium heat until sugar dissolves.

5 With an adult's help, add the strips of peel to the syrup mixture. Turn the heat as low as possible and simmer, partially covered, for forty-five to sixty minutes. To test doneness, peels should be soft and should have absorbed most of the syrup mixture. Turn off burner and allow peels to cool in the saucepan.

6 Place a sheet of heavy-duty aluminum foil on your work surface. When peels have cooled, spread them in a single layer on the foil so that they are flat and not touching each other. Make sure the grapefruit skin is facing up. Allow them to cool completely, then sprinkle them with the remaining ½ cup sugar. Let them stand, uncovered, until they are completely dry, about five to seven hours or overnight, if possible. Store the skin in a tightly closed container.

Makes: About 2 pounds of dermatologists' delights

Colorful Wormie Skin Squares

The worms crawl in, the worms crawl out, they eat the flesh then spit it out . . . for you and your friends to consume!

INGREDIENTS

2 12-ounce bags white chocolate
chips

1 14-ounce can sweetened condensed milk

⅛ teaspoon salt

1 ½ teaspoons vanilla extract

1 cup Gummi Worms®

TOOLS YOU'LL NEED

• 9-inch square pan • waxed paper • medium-sized heavy saucepan
• wooden spoon • pot holder • cutting board • large knife

1 Line a 9-inch square pan with waxed paper and set aside.

2 Place white chocolate, sweetened condensed milk, and salt together in a medium-sized heavy saucepan. With an adult's help, heat mixture over medium heat, stirring constantly with a wooden spoon, until chips are melted. Use a pot holder to hold the pan steady. Stir in vanilla and remove from heat.

3 With an adult's help, pour white chocolate mixture into square pan. Evenly lay Gummi Worms® over skin and place pan in refrigerator. Chill for at least two hours or until firm.

4 When set, turn worm-infested skin onto a cutting board. Peel away waxed paper lining. Ask an adult to help you cut the worm-infested skin into 1-inch squares with the large cutting knife.

Makes: 2 ¼ pounds of sweet infested flesh

PUTRID PRESENTATION

If you'd like to create ethnically diverse rotting flesh, substitute one of the 12-ounce bags of white chocolate chips for butterscotch- flavored chips to create Hispanic skin. To make African-American skin, replace the white chocolate chips with milk chocolate or semi-sweet chocolate chips.

CONTAMINATED COOKIES

Crusty
Belly
Buttons
(page 38)

Congealed
Cat Guts
(page 40)

Used
Bandages
(page 36)

Toilet Paper Wads

*It's a wipeout! Make your friends a wad of cookies
they'll go bottoms up for!*

INGREDIENTS

4 eggs

½ teaspoon cream of tartar

1 cup granulated sugar

1 teaspoon vanilla

1 cup mini marshmallows

½ cup chocolate sauce

TOOLS YOU'LL NEED

- 2 small bowls • large mixing bowl • electric mixer
- rubber spatula • greased baking sheet • pot holders
- wire rack • flat metal spatula • 1-inch paintbrush

1 Ask an adult to help you preheat the oven to 200 degrees.

2 When separating eggs, it is very important to start with a clean and totally dry bowl. To separate eggs, gently but firmly crack the egg against the rim of your small bowl. Carefully rock the yolk back and forth in the shell while you allow the whites to fall into the bowl. After separating, place yolks in a second small bowl, and reserve them for another use. As you separate each egg, place egg whites in a large mixing bowl. (It's a good idea to separate each egg in a small bowl first so you don't ruin the whole batch of whites should a bit of yolk fall in.)

3 With an adult's help, beat whites with an electric mixer on medium speed until foamy. Add cream of tartar and beat until egg whites begin to hold peaks when you lift beaters.

Turn the mixer to high speed and begin to add sugar very slowly—about 1 teaspoon at a time, beating well after each spoonful. When you're finished, egg whites should hold stiff, shiny peaks when you lift beaters.

4 Add vanilla and beat briefly to mix. Add marshmallows and gently fold them in with a rubber spatula.

5 Drop meringue mixture by heaping tablespoonfuls onto greased baking sheet about 1 inch apart.

6 Using pot holders, ask an adult to help you place the toilet paper wads in the oven. Bake for about an hour, until cookies are dry to the touch. They should not turn brown while baking, so keep an eye on them.

7 With an adult's help, use pot holders to remove baking sheet from oven and place sheet directly on wire rack to cool for about 10 minutes. Then transfer wads directly to wire rack using a flat metal spatula.

8 When wads have cooled completely, dip a clean 1-inch paintbrush into the chocolate sauce and wipe one stripe directly down the center of eachwad just before serving.

Makes: About 36 flushable (and edible) wads

31

Road-Kill Bar Cookies

Bring along a batch of these for your family's next road trip. Then, if you run out, be on the lookout for critters crossin' where they ought not to!

INGREDIENTS

1 20-ounce package refrigerated peanut butter cookie dough

1 12-ounce package semi-sweet chocolate chips

2 tablespoons butter

1 14-ounce can sweetened condensed milk

2 teaspoons vanilla extract

ready-made decorating frosting in yellow and red

16 unfrosted animal cookies

TOOLS YOU'LL NEED

- 13 by 9 by 2-inch baking pan, greased and floured
- pot holders • medium-sized, heavy saucepan
- wooden spoon • rubber spatula • utility knife
- flat metal spatula • waxed paper

1 With an adult's help, preheat oven to 350 degrees (325 degrees for glass dishes).

2 With floured hands, press cookie dough on the bottom of greased and floured baking pan to form a flat, even crust. Wear pot holders and ask an adult to help you place pan in the oven. Bake fifteen to twenty minutes or until golden. Ask an adult to help you remove it from the oven and place it on a heat-safe surface to cool completely.

3 Place semi-sweet chocolate chips, butter, sweetened condensed milk, and vanilla in a medium-sized heavy saucepan. With an adult's help, cook the mixture over medium heat until chips are completely melted. Use pot holders to hold

the pan steady. Stir occasionally with a wooden spoon. Continue to heat and stir until mixture is thickened, about five minutes. Carefully spread the melted mixture over cooled cookie crust with a rubber spatula. Chill in the refrigerator for about an hour.

4 With an adult's help, use a utility knife to cut out sixteen rectangle-shaped cookies (pieces of road). Cut four evenly spaced slices lengthwise and widthwise into the pan. Remove pieces from pan with a flat metal spatula and place them on a sheet of waxed paper.

5 To decorate, use the ready-made decorating frosting to draw a double yellow line lengthwise down the center of each cookie square to form divided roads. Next, squirt a dime-sized dot of red frosting (blood) near the center of the road and place one animal cookie on the center of each dot and press firmly down so that blood squirts out the sides of the road kill. Serve immediately or store loosely at room temperature.

Makes: 16 highway hits

PUTRID PRESENTATION

Souvenirs from your recent road trip will make an ideal gift idea! Cut up an old map (be sure to check with the folks first!) and use it to line your serving platter and to show where you've been gathering your gifts.

Used Bandages

These scab-filled treats are a cut above! Not only do they cover up your oozing wounds, they do double duty as a sweet "pick-me-up"!

INGREDIENTS

10 large graham crackers
1 raspberry or strawberry fruit
  roll-up
20 large marshmallows

6 tablespoons milk
2 teaspoons vanilla
2 cups confectioners' sugar
orange food coloring

TOOLS YOU'LL NEED

• utility knife • 4-cup microwave-safe glass measuring cup
• rubber spatula

1 Break the graham crackers into fourths along each cracker's perforated lines. Set aside. Unroll the fruit roll-up and tear off forty dime-sized pieces to be used as scabs. Set them aside as well.

2 With an adult's help, use the utility knife to cut marshmallows in half, widthwise. Then cut the rounded edges off the sides of the marshmallow halves to form a square gauze for the bandage. Set aside.

3 Place milk and vanilla in the microwave-safe glass measuring cup. With an adult's help, place measuring cup in the microwave and heat on high for about twenty seconds or until milk is hot.

4 With an adult's help, remove the measuring cup from the microwave and pour in confectioners' sugar. Mix quickly with a rubber spatula until fully blended and smooth. Add two to three drops of orange food coloring and mix thoroughly until you've achieved a classic "bandage peach" tone.

5 To assemble, use the rubber spatula to frost each graham cracker. Frosting should be thin enough to allow cracker's dimples to show through. (If frosting is too thick, add more warm milk.) Next, gently press marshmallows down, one on the center of each graham cracker, sticky side down toward the cracker. Next, dip the tip of your clean finger in water to moisten, then rub it on one side of a fruit roll piece. Center one scab, wet side down, on each bandage.

Makes: 40 cookie cuts

PUTRID PRESENTATION

Simply reserve a small amount of frosting and color it with one drop of green to create a realistic pus shade. Then dab about ⅛ teaspoon on the top of each gauze pad before you put down the scab. (Let the pus ooze out from beneath the scab!)

Crusty Belly Buttons

Stinky, smelly, and full of crust,
these dirty belly buttons are a must!

INGREDIENTS

2 ½ cups all-purpose flour
½ teaspoon baking powder
⅛ teaspoon salt
1 cup butter

1 cup granulated sugar
1 large egg
1 teaspoon vanilla
1 cup orange marmalade

TOOLS YOU'LL NEED

• medium mixing bowl • large mixing bowl • electric mixer
• baking sheet • pot holders • flat metal spatula • wire rack

1 With an adult's help, preheat oven to 325 degrees. Place flour, baking powder, and salt in a medium mixing bowl. Set aside.

2 Place butter and sugar in a large mixing bowl. With an adult's help, use electric mixer to blend until creamy. Add egg and vanilla and continue beating. Gradually blend in flour mixture until well blended, smooth, and firm.

3 To shape a natural-looking belly button, scoop 1 tablespoon of dough into your clean, dry hands. Roll dough back and forth in the palms of your hands to form a ball. Place the ball on the ungreased baking sheet.

4 To create the hollow of your belly button, use your index finger knuckle and press firmly down in the center of dough. (Be careful not to go all the way through to the baking sheet.) Next, pinch the outer sides of each dough ball. Skin folds will be formed in the center. Then, without letting go, press the pinched-out pieces of dough gently back against the cookie's sides to create the belly button. Fill the hollow with ¼ teaspoon of orange marmalade. Repeat with remaining dough and marmalade.

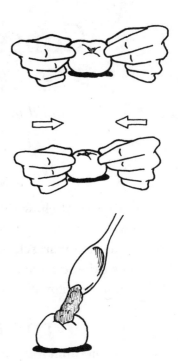

5   Use pot holders and ask an adult to help you place baking sheet in the oven. Bake for 18 to 22 minutes or until light golden brown. Remove them from the oven and use a flat metal spatula to transfer belly buttons to a wire rack to cool.

Makes: 48 juice-filled innie belly buttons

Congealed Cat Guts

You'll love getting your claws into this
purr-fectly disgusting treat!

INGREDIENTS

1 5-ounce can of chow mein noodles

½ cup candied maraschino cherries or dried cranberries

1 cup mini marshmallows

½ cup white chocolate chips

12 ounces red candy-making chocolate

1 14-ounce can sweetened condensed milk

TOOLS YOU'LL NEED

- medium mixing bowl • baking sheet • waxed paper
- large microwave-safe bowl • plastic wrap • pot holders
- large wooden spoon • utility spoon

1 Place chow mein noodles, candied maraschino cherries or dried cranberries, marshmallows, and white chocolate chips into a medium-sized bowl and mix well. Set aside.

2 Clear a space in the refrigerator big enough for you to place a baking sheet. Line the baking sheet with waxed paper and set aside.

3 Place red candy-making chocolate and sweetened condensed milk into large microwave-safe bowl. Cover lightly with plastic wrap. With an adult's help, microwave on high for about 1½ minutes. Use pot holders to remove bowl from

microwave. Stir well with a large wooden spoon. Cover and return to the microwave. Cook on high for approximately 1½ minutes and stir again. Use pot holders to place the bowl on a work surface.

4 Immediately pour the chow mein noodle mixture into the melted chocolate. Stir with a utility spoon to coat well.

5 Use a tablespoon to drop scoops of cat guts onto lined baking sheet. Chill about an hour (or until firm) in the refrigerator.

Makes: About 36 gut-wrenching goodies

PUTRID PRESENTATION

At your next party, give these cat guts road-kill flair. Run a strip of black construction paper down the center of your table to look like a street. Paint a double yellow line down the center of the paper with nontoxic poster paint. Proudly place the guts in strategic places along the road.

RANCID REFRESHMENTS

Saliva Slurp
(page 42)

Mister Blue's
Toilet Bowl
Punch
(page 46)

Frozen
Water
Blisters
(page 50)

Old Mold Malt
(page 44)

Saliva Slurp

Now here's a drink worth drooling over.

INGREDIENTS

1 envelope unflavored gelatin

1 6-ounce can frozen lemonade
  concentrate

40 ice cubes or 4 cups crushed
  ice

2 cups chilled club soda

TOOLS YOU'LL NEED

• baking sheet • waxed paper • microwave-safe cup
• fork • blender • 4 tall glasses • 4 straws

1 Line baking sheet with waxed paper. Set aside. To create saliva, empty unflavored gelatin into a microwave-safe cup and follow package's microwave directions for dissolving gelatin. Place cup in the refrigerator for fifteen minutes to set.

2 Then stir the gelatin vigorously with a fork to put air bubbles in the mixture. Drop by tablespoonfuls onto lined baking sheet about 2 inches apart so that saliva blobs don't run together. (Make sure you've got a dollop of saliva for each glass!)

3 Return saliva-filled baking sheet to the refrigerator to continue setting for about ten minutes. Then peel saliva blobs away from waxed paper and line the rim of each glass with a glob of saliva.

4 Pour frozen lemonade concentrate, ice cubes, and club soda into blender, and with an adult's help, blend on high for about a minute or until ice cubes are finely chopped.

5 Immediately pour the mixture into glasses. Serve with straws.

Serves: 4 drooling dudes

PUTRID PRESENTATION

Show your guests how fresh your saliva really is. Drool as you're serving!

Mister Blue's Toilet Bowl Punch

Don't rush to flush! Bet you didn't know how tasty
that pretty blue toilet bowl water can be.

INGREDIENTS

16 bite-size chocolates, such as
  Hershey's Kisses®
1½ cups water
1 6-ounce box blueberry gelatin

1 6-ounce can fresh frozen
  pineapple juice concentrate*
1 quart chilled sparkling mineral
  water
2 quarts chilled lemon-lime soda

* (Using fresh or fresh frozen pineapple juice will prevent the gelatin from setting and
  keep it liquid. Do NOT use canned pineapple juice!)

TOOLS YOU'LL NEED

• ice-cube tray • medium-sized saucepan • wooden spoon
• plastic wrap • 4-cup glass measuring cup
• 4-quart ceramic bowl (or any 4-quart punch bowl)
• ladle • cups

1 Unwrap chocolates and place one in each section of the ice-cube tray. Set aside. With an adult's help, bring 1½ cups water to boil in a medium-sized saucepan. Use pot holders to remove pan from heat and place on a heat-safe work surface. Pour in blueberry gelatin and stir with a wooden spoon to dissolve completely. Pour in pineapple juice (must be

fresh frozen concentrate!) and continue stirring until mixture is thoroughly blended. Cover with plastic wrap and chill in the refrigerator.

2   After it reaches room temperature, pour ¾ cup blueberry gelatin mixture into a 4-cup glass measuring cup. Add enough water to bring the level up to 2 cups. (This should be enough to fill the ice-cube tray. If yours requires more, add enough additional water so that this mixture will cover the chocolates.) Place tray in the freezer compartment until ice cubes are formed, about two hours.

3   Pour gelatin mixture into the large bowl. Add remaining ingredients and mix thoroughly. Empty poop-filled ice cubes into punch (toilet) bowl and serve immediately.

Serves: 16 sewage slurpers

PUTRID PRESENTATION

Add a touch of class when you're serving this great grog and pass out coasters made of folded-up toilet tissue! In advance, fold squares about four layers thick, one for each glass. Then get a brown felt-tip marker and draw a thick stripe down the center.

Backwashed Banana Shake

Chew it, swallow it, spit it back out! Bananas are nice when you've eaten them twice.

INGREDIENTS

2 large ripe bananas
1 14-ounce can sweetened con-
    densed milk
1 cup cold water
⅓ cup concentrated or fresh
    lemon juice

2 teaspoons vanilla
2 cups ice cubes
½ cup large curd cottage cheese
½ cup mini multicolored
    marshmallows

TOOLS YOU'LL NEED

• small mixing bowl • fork • blender
• 3 or 4 tall glasses • 3 or 4 long iced-tea spoons or straws

1   Place bananas in a small mixing bowl and use a fork to mash bananas to a lumpy consistency. Set aside.

2   With an adult's help, pour sweetened condensed milk, water, lemon juice, and vanilla into blender. Place the lid on and mix thoroughly on high. Gradually add ice cubes and continue blending until ice is thoroughly crushed.

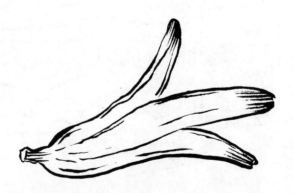

3 Add the mashed bananas, cottage cheese, and mini marshmallows, and with an adult's help, mix on low speed for about ten seconds. (Mix just enough to blend ingredients—you want the consistency to remain just-chewed and chunky!) Pour into tall glasses and serve with straws or iced-tea spoons.

Serves: 3 to 4 backwashing buddies

PUTRID PRESENTATION

Backwashed Banana Shakes are a great way to wash down Chocolate Armpit Hairs, page 12.

Frozen Water Blisters

Kick up your heels! Here's a dessert that'll turn ordinary water blisters into refreshing treats the whole family will enjoy.

INGREDIENTS

4 to 6 medium-sized lemons (enough to make ½ cup lemon juice)

3 tablespoons grated lemon zest (the yellow part of the peel only)

3 cups whipping cream

1 ½ cups granulated sugar

TOOLS YOU'LL NEED

• grater • vegetable peeler • utility knife • citrus juicer
• large bowl • wire whisk • cupcake pan
• utility spoon • aluminum foil

1 For this recipe, you will use peeled and hollowed lemon halves to create your giant blister skins. First you have to remove the bright yellow outermost portion of peel, the zest, so that only the thick white portion of peel, the pith, remains. With an adult's help, grate lemon peel, then use a vegetable peeler to remove any remaining zest from lemons.

2 Next, ask an adult to help you cut the lemons in half, with the lemon tip on the bottom of each half. Then carefully slice off the pointed tips just so that the halves set flat.

3 Juice all the lemon halves, using your citrus juicer, so that just the white pith remains. Set aside. You need ½ cup lemon juice. Reserve any additional juice for use later.

4 With an adult's help, pour whipping cream, lemon juice, and sugar into a large bowl and stir with a wire whisk until thoroughly blended.

5 To hold the lemon halves (blister skins) upright, place them in your cupcake pan so that the openings face upward, like a cup. Then pour blister filling evenly among the lemon halves using a utility spoon. Fill each one about ¾ full. Cover with foil and freeze overnight. To serve, put each Frozen Water Blister in a separate small bowl, and pass it out— along with a spoon—to your guests.

Makes: 8 to 12 chilly boils

PUTRID PRESENTATION

Plan on serving these to the team after your next softball game. Then gather your team- mates and compare blisters. Give an award to the biggest, grossest blister!

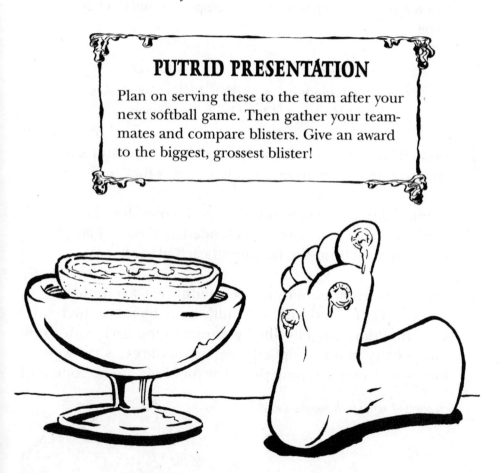

Old Mold Malt

Is the expiration date on your dairy products from another decade? Don't clean that refrigerator just yet! When it comes to mold, the older the better for this malt mixture!

INGREDIENTS

½ cup flaked coconut

¾ cup green mint jelly

1½ cups ready-made whipped topping

2 pints vanilla ice cream

2 cups buttermilk

1 teaspoon vanilla extract

TOOLS YOU'LL NEED

• small mixing bowl • fork • 4 tall clear glasses
• blender • 4 long iced-tea spoons

1 Place flaked coconut in the small mixing bowl and add 4 tablespoons of the green mint jelly. Use a fork to mix.

2 When flakes have taken on a greenish color, fold in whipped topping until color is slightly blended. Set aside. Place 2 tablespoons jelly at the bottom of each glass. Set aside.

3 Place ice cream, buttermilk, and vanilla extract in the blender. Cover, and with an adult's help, blend on high until smooth. Pour into jelly-filled glasses and top each with a dollop of hairy mold (whipped topping mixture). Serve with long spoons for scraping that tasty mold off the bottom, too!

Serves: 4 untidy housekeepers

QUEASY CAKES & UNPALATABLE PIES

Sweet Escargot
(page 58)

Open Wound
Teacakes
(page 62)

Dead Rat Cupcakes
(page 60)

Squid Tentacles Torte

Live and still moving, squiggly squid tentacles will tickle your taste buds.

INGREDIENTS

1 box yellow cake mix (plus those ingredients listed on package)

1¼ cups water

1 3-ounce package grape or blueberry gelatin

purple food coloring

5¼ cups (12 ounces) ready-made whipped topping

1½ cups Froot Loops® (purple loops only)

1 cup boysenberry syrup

TOOLS YOU'LL NEED

- 2 9-inch round cake pans, greased and floured
- electric mixer • large mixing bowl • rubber spatula
- toothpick • wire rack • large fork • small saucepan
- pot holders • cake plate

1 With an adult's help, preheat oven to the temperature shown on the cake mix package.

2 Prepare cake mix according to package directions. Ask an adult to help you if you're using a mixer. With an adult's help, bake the cake according to the directions on the package for two 9-inch round cake pans. The cakes are done when a toothpick inserted into the center of cakes comes out clean. When they have begun to cool, remove the cakes from baking pans by inverting them onto a wire rack.

3 Wash and dry cake pans. After cakes have cooled completely, put pans back over each baked cake and carefully turn them over so that cakes are back in pans with the rounded baked tops facing up once again. Poke a large fork into each cake round several times. Make each set of holes about ¾-inch apart. Set cakes aside.

4 With an adult's help, bring 1¼ cups water to boil in saucepan. Using pot holders, remove from heat and place on a heat-safe work surface. Pour in gelatin and use your fork to stir until completely dissolved. When gelatin has cooled slightly, have an adult pour it evenly over both cakes. Place them in the refrigerator to chill for at least three hours or until firm.

5 Drop six to ten drops of purple food coloring into ready-made whipped topping container and use a rubber spatula to carefully blend in color. Return colored whipped topping to the refrigerator until you are ready to use.

6 When tentacles have set, remove pans from the refrigerator. Fill the kitchen sink with 1 to 2 inches of warm water. Carefully dip the cake pans into the warm water to loosen and unmold cakes from pans. Do not allow water to go over the pans and onto your cakes.

7 Place the first layer onto the center of a cake plate and frost the tops and sides with purple whipped topping, using a rubber spatula. Next, with an adult's help, place the second

layer on top of the first and frost top and sides with remaining whipped topping.

8 Evenly space purple Froot Loops® (squid's suction cups) all around the squid cake.

9 Squids squirt out black ink when they're in danger. Just before serving, give each dessert plate a realistic ink squirt by splattering it with 2 or 3 tablespoons of boysenberry syrup.

Serves: About 12 fishy friends

Bessie's Homemade Cow Pie

Guests in the mooood for a truly unique treat? Put 'em out to pasture, then shovel up a fresh, steamy plop—one for every plate!

INGREDIENTS

FOR DECORATING:
1 cup coconut flakes
¼ teaspoon milk
green food coloring

FOR CRUST:
about 30 chocolate cookies
¼ cup granulated sugar
¼ cup butter or margarine

FOR PIE:
1 8-ounce package cream cheese, softened
1 cup chunky peanut butter
1 cup granulated sugar
1 tablespoon butter or margarine, softened
1 teaspoon vanilla extract
2 ½ cups ready-made whipped topping

TOOLS YOU'LL NEED

• small mixing bowl • fork • baking sheet • pot holders
• 1 gallon plastic bag • rolling pin • microwave-safe measuring cup
• medium mixing bowl • large mixing bowl
• electric mixer • rubber spatula

1 Place ½ cup coconut flakes (reserve the rest for toasting) into a small mixing bowl. Add milk and a few drops green food coloring. With a fork, mix the color thoroughly. Set aside.

2 With an adult's help, preheat oven to 350 degrees. Spread remaining ½ cup coconut flakes evenly onto the baking sheet. Place baking sheet in oven and bake for about two minutes. With an adult's help, use pot holders to remove the

sheet from the oven and place it on a heat-safe work surface. Stir it with the clean fork in order to toast coconut
evenly. Return baking sheet to the oven for a total bake time
of about twelve minutes or until coconut is lightly browned.
Set aside. Do not turn oven off, as you'll need it at this same
temperature to bake the cow-pie crust.

3   Place chocolate cookies into a gallon plastic bag and seal
with a twist tie or zip it closed. Be sure to remove air pockets
from the bag, so that the bag is flat. Place it on your work
surface and firmly roll over cookies with rolling pin to thoroughly crush cookies into crumbs.

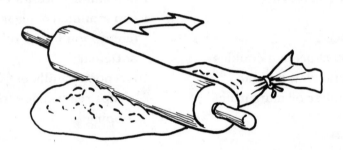

4   Next, place butter or margarine in a microwave safe measuring cup, put it in the microwave, and heat on high for about
thirty seconds or until melted. Have an adult help you
remove measuring cup from the microwave. Pour ¼ cup
melted butter or margarine, ¼ cup sugar, and 1¼ cups
cookie crumbs into a medium-sized mixing bowl and mix
thoroughly with a fork.

5   Pour crumb mixture into a 9-inch pie plate and press down
firmly to form a cow-pie crust. With an adult's help, use pot
holders to place the pie crust in the oven and bake for ten
minutes. Remove crust from the oven and allow it to cool
completely on a heat-safe work surface.

6 Place cream cheese in a large mixing bowl. With an adult's help, beat cream cheese with an electric mixer to soften. Add in chunky peanut butter, 1 cup sugar, 1 tablespoon butter or margarine, and vanilla extract. Beat until thoroughly blended. Fold in ready-made whipped topping.

7 Use a rubber spatula to spoon bowl's contents into the cooled pie crust. Spread evenly. To decorate, sprinkle remaining cookie crumbs onto cow-pie edges as dirt. Then sprinkle green coconut (Bessie's freshly chewed clover) in the center, up to the dirt edge. Finally, sprinkle toasted coconut (clover that's already been through the digestive track) evenly over entire pie.

Serves: 8 to 10 "udderly" grossed-out guests

PUTRID PRESENTATION

Make several smaller cow plops and host a cow-pie eating contest! Have guests hold their hands behind them and dig in—face first!

Sweet Escargot

Are your friends a little sluggish? Head out to the garden and dig up a dessert you know they'll love!

INGREDIENTS

1 black licorice lace

1 8-ounce roll ready-made refrigerated cinnamon roll dough

8 green gumdrops

TOOLS YOU'LL NEED

- kitchen scissors • baking sheet
- 16 toothpicks • pot holders

1   With an adult's help, preheat oven as directed on package of cinnamon rolls. Snip licorice lace into sixteen 1-inch snips to be used later as antennae. Set aside.

2   Open dough package. Cinnamon roll dough comes pre-wound in a spiral pattern. Unwind about 3 inches of dough. Bend that dough back upon itself as if you are unwinding the spiral. Note: After baking, you will insert your snail's gumdrop head into this fold.

3   Next, press the spiral onto its side, with folded-over dough portion facing forward, so that swirls are visible on either side. Then press dough down slightly onto the ungreased baking sheet so that the snail has a flat base. Prop up each side with a toothpick. Repeat until all the

dough is used up. Ask an adult to help you bake as directed on package. With an adult's help, wear pot holders and remove baking sheet from oven. Allow slugs to cool on baking sheet.

4 When slugs have cooled enough to handle, carefully remove toothpicks. Gently wedge one gumdrop head into each folded-over portion of baked snail (cinnamon roll). Insert two antennae into the head of each snail. Drizzle both sides of each snail with enclosed frosting package and serve.

Serves: 8 slug munchers

PUTRID PRESENTATION

Pick up small terra-cotta pots at your local garden shop and wash and rinse them thoroughly. Cover the drain hole with waxed paper. Then fill them with instant chocolate pudding. Top off each pot with crushed chocolate cookie crumbs as dirt. When serving your snails, place one in the center of each flower pot. A gardener's delight!

Dead Rat Cupcakes

Rodent tails are truly disgusting, but their yummy flavor will surely trap you!

INGREDIENTS

1 box cake mix, any flavor (plus those ingredients listed on package)

black food coloring (found at baking supply stores or create your own from colors you have)

1 16-ounce can ready-made vanilla frosting

1 black licorice lace

red gumdrops or red cherry balls (two per cupcake)

chocolate chips (one per cupcake)

dime-sized flat, round thin mint wafers (two for each cupcake)

small tube ready-made red decorating frosting

TOOLS YOU'LL NEED

- standard cupcake pan • paper cupcake liners • kitchen scissors
- gray pipe cleaners (one for each cupcake) • rubber spatula

1 With an adult's help, preheat the oven according to the "cupcake baking" directions on the cake mix package. Line the cupcake tins with paper liners and set aside. Use kitchen scissors to snip licorice laces into ½-inch-long snips for whiskers and set aside. You should have about four whiskers per rat. Fold a pipe cleaner into a squared-off "U" shape (a rectangle with three sides) for use as a rat trap hinge. Make one for each cupcake.

2 With an adult's help, prepare and bake cupcakes as directed on the package. Allow cupcakes to cool completely before decorating.

3 Use a rubber spatula to blend a few drops of black food coloring into the frosting container. Create a dark gray color, like an alley rat. Frost cupcakes evenly.

4 To create truly lifelike dead rats, place two red gumdrops or cherry balls on frosted cupcake tops as eyes, one chocolate chip in the center as each rat's nose. Then wedge two dime-sized round, flat thin mints into each cupcake as ears. Next, insert four licorice whiskers around each rat's nose. Finally, poke a U-shaped pipe cleaner firmly into the sides of each rat's head just below the ears and squirt two dots of red decorating frosting at the base of the rat-trap hinge, right where it has impaled the dead rat.

Serves: 12 to 16 rat attackers

PUTRID PRESENTATION

Make your pals reach into a dirty "rat hole" if they're hungry for a treat! To create the rat-sized hiding place, use an old shoe box and brown crate paper. Crumple paper into balls, then smooth it back out. Wrap shoe box with the crumpled paper. Cut two large holes, one on each narrow end, for your hands to fit through. Your guests will have to reach inside the dead rat's hiding place if they want dessert.

Open Wound Teacakes

Here's a batch of boo-boos they'll love to lick.

INGREDIENTS

32 wrapped hard red candies
(about 8 ounces)

1 18-ounce roll ready-made refrigerated sugar cookie dough

½ cup flour

TOOLS YOU'LL NEED

• baking sheet • waxed paper • butter knife • rolling pin
• 3-inch round cookie cutter • pot holders
• flat metal spatula • wire rack

1   With an adult's help, preheat the oven as directed on cookie dough package. Line baking sheet with waxed paper and set aside. Unwrap candies and set aside.

2   Ask an adult to help you use the butter knife to slice dough into ½-inch-thick rounds. Rub flour on your rolling pin, then roll each dough wedge to about ¼ inch thickness. Next, use the cookie cutter to make sixteen to eighteen circles.

3   Then cut individually shaped gashes and wound openings into each cookie dough circle using the butter knife. Ask an adult to help you with the knife. Each wound should be uniquely shaped and no bigger than 2 to 3 inches around. Jagged edges

made randomly with the butter knife on the inner circle will make wounds look true to life!

4 Carefully place wounds on lined baking sheet about 2 inches apart. With an adult's help, use pot holders to place baking sheet into the oven and bake for about seven minutes. Carefully remove sheet from oven, but do not turn oven off.

5 Have an adult help you carefully place two hard candies in the center of each wound. Return baking sheet to the oven and continue baking for three to five minutes, until the hard candies have melted into fresh bloody wound openings.

6 Cool the teacakes on the trays for about three minutes, then use a flat metal spatula to carefully transfer them to a wire rack to cool completely.

*Makes: 16 to 18
bleeding biscuits*

PUTRID PRESENTATION

Don't forget the anti-bacterial ointment! Serve open wounds with a bowl of honey for dipping so guests can prevent infections and enjoy soothing relief.

Blood Clot Cake

*Serve up a heart-attack sized helping
to all your guests!*

INGREDIENTS

¼ cup butter or margarine

4 cups day-old French or sour-
dough bread (broken into
1-inch pieces)

3 eggs

2 cups milk

½ cup granulated sugar

2 teaspoons vanilla extract

½ teaspoon ground cinnamon

½ teaspoon ground nutmeg

½ teaspoon salt

red food coloring

1 cup fresh raspberries

FOR BLOOD SAUCE:

3 tablespoons butter or
margarine

2 tablespoons sugar

1 tablespoon cornstarch

¾ cup milk

¼ cup grenadine syrup

1 teaspoon vanilla extract

TOOLS YOU'LL NEED

- microwave-safe glass measuring cup
- 2-quart casserole dish, greased • wooden spoon
- medium mixing bowl • wire whisk • pot holders
- butter knife • small saucepan • small mixing bowl • fork

1 With an adult's help, place butter or margarine in a
microwave-safe measuring cup and heat it on high for about
30 seconds or until melted. Set aside. Preheat oven to 350
degrees.

2   Fill prepared casserole dish with bread cubes and cover with the melted butter. Use a wooden spoon to toss and coat bread cubes evenly. Set aside.

3   In a medium mixing bowl, whisk together eggs, milk, sugar, vanilla, cinnamon, nutmeg, salt, and enough red food coloring to make the mixture a nice shade of blood red. Stir in raspberries and pour entire mixture over bread cubes. Stir gently with the wooden spoon to coat.

4   With an adult's help, use pot holders and place casserole in the oven. Bake for about forty minutes or until a butter knife inserted in the center comes out clean.

5   While clot cake is baking, prepare warm blood sauce. Have an adult help you melt butter or margarine in a small saucepan. Combine sugar and cornstarch in a small mixing bowl, and stir with a fork. Then add it to the melted butter. Stir in milk and grenadine syrup. Continue to cook and stir

with the fork over a medium heat until mixture comes to a full boil. Boil for one minute. Carefully remove from the heat and stir in vanilla. Set aside until clot cake has finished baking and is cool enough to handle.

6 Just before serving, have an adult help you cut clots into six equal portions. Pour warm blood over each clot square and serve.

Serves: 6 clot chewers

PUTRID PRESENTATION

Get guests into the party "flow" by handing out handmade "artery accessories" as party favors. Start with several long, very skinny dark purple balloons (the type clowns use for making balloon animals). Fill them with water, making sure they keep their long, thin shapes. Tie them off to keep water inside. Then tie them into small loops as artery bracelets or tie a few together as artery necklaces. Soak arteries in warm water before you pass them out so they'll have a wet, warm vein-like feeling!

THE GROSSER GOURMET

Dead Roach Torte Surprise (page 78)

Poached Seagull Droppings (page 76)

Toe Jam Fondue (page 68)

Toe Jam Fondue

*Love to scrape out that gooey, sweaty, stinky stuff between your toes?
Then taste "de-feet" and enjoy true culinary success.*

INGREDIENTS

4 golden delicious apples
(or other light-skinned yellow-ish apples)
1 lemon

¾ cup chunky peanut butter
½ cup pancake syrup
¼ cup large curd cottage cheese

TOOLS YOU'LL NEED

• utility knife • vegetable peeler • medium serving bowl
• kitchen tablespoon • small microwave-safe serving bowl
• fork • pot holders

1 Wash apples and remove stems. Ask an adult to help you cut each apple lengthwise into four quarters. You should have sixteen finger-length apple wedges. Next, slice lemon in half and squeeze one of the halves over the apple wedges. Lemon juice will help prevent the apples from turning brown.

2 Have an adult help you carve out giant toes with your vegetable peeler. First, peel away apple cores and seeds. Then peel the skin from the lower, narrow two thirds of each apple wedge. Leave the top portion of apple skin on to resemble a fungus-infested

nail. Finally, use the peeler to round out and shape the toe's tip and edges. Place toes in the serving bowl and squeeze remaining lemon half onto toes. Gently toss with a kitchen tablespoon to coat thoroughly with juice.

3 Place peanut butter and pancake syrup in your small microwave-safe serving bowl. With a fork, thoroughly mix ingredients.

4 Put bowl in microwave and, with an adult's help, heat on high for thirty to forty seconds or until mixture is warm. Using pot holders, carefully remove from microwave and stir in large curd cottage cheese. Immediately place warm fondue near the serving bowl of big toes. Now everyone can easily dip their digits into the tasty toe jam!

Serves: 4 little piggies

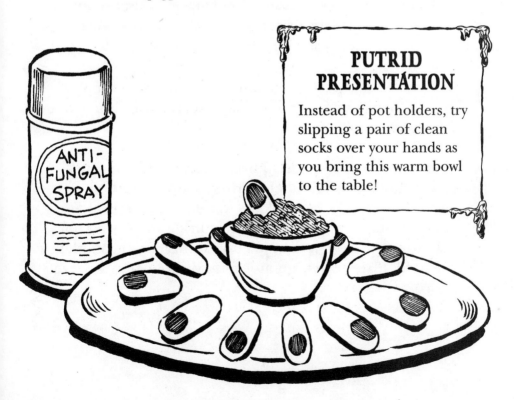

PUTRID PRESENTATION

Instead of pot holders, try slipping a pair of clean socks over your hands as you bring this warm bowl to the table!

Bloody Nose Soup

Next time you get a nosebleed, don't tilt your head back, tilt it forward and let it run into your serving bowls!

INGREDIENTS

1 20-ounce bag frozen raspberries, thawed
1¼ cups water
1 cup cran-raspberry juice
½ cup granulated sugar

1½ teaspoons ground cinnamon
3 whole cloves
1 tablespoon lemon juice
½ cup sour cream

TOOLS YOU'LL NEED

• blender • large saucepan • pot holders • large strainer
• large heat-safe serving bowl • wire whisk • ladle
• 4 to 6 small serving bowls • kitchen tablespoon

1 With an adult's help, pour raspberries and water into blender container, put lid on, and puree. Pour into a large saucepan.

2 Add in the cran-raspberry juice, sugar, cinnamon, and cloves. With an adult's help, bring mixture to a boil over medium heat. Use pot holders to remove from heat and pour through a strainer and into a heat-safe serving bowl. Allow to cool. Add lemon juice and whisk until completely blended. Place in refrigerator until you're ready to serve.

3 Just before serving, ladle bloody nose soup into bowls. Use a kitchen tablespoon to drop dollops of sour cream (cotton balls) onto the center of each bowl of bloody nose soup. Serve chilled.

Serves: 4 to 6 nosy neighbors

PUTRID PRESENTATION

Squirt red frosting so that it appears to be dripping out of your nostrils. Then serve the soup as if there's nothing wrong. When everyone lets you know your nose is bleeding, just wipe it off and eat it. Explain that it's sometimes hard to make the bleeding stop after you're finished filling the bowls.

Placenta Bombe

(pluh-sen-tuh bahm-boh)

Skip the after-dinner mints, after-birth is much more special!
Serve one up at your next birthday bash!

INGREDIENTS

1 pound-cake loaf (about 12 ounces)

2 16-ounce cans jellied cranberries

2½ cups cold milk

2 packages (3.4 ounces each) instant chocolate pudding and pie filling

2 cups ready-made whipped topping

TOOLS YOU'LL NEED

- large serrated knife • 2-quart bowl • plastic wrap
- can opener • large mixing bowl • wire whisk
- rubber spatula • serving platter

1 With an adult's help, use a serrated knife to cut pound cake into about fourteen very thin slices. Set aside. Line the inside of a 2-quart bowl with plastic wrap and set aside. Open jellied cranberry cans and gently shake contents onto your work surface, making sure they keep the round can shape. (Jellied cranberries have the consistency of gelatin.) Slice each jelly roll into eight equal slices. Set aside.

2 Pour milk into a large mixing bowl and add pudding mix. Beat with a whisk until well blended, about one to two minutes. Let pudding mixture stand for about five minutes. Fold in ½ of the ready-made whipped topping mix with a rubber spatula.

3 To build the placenta, arrange half of the jellied cranberry slices on the bottom and sides of lined bowl, pushing slices as close together as possible. Spread about a third of the pudding mixture over cranberry slices in bowl using your rubber spatula. Place about six cake slices over pudding layer and press down gently. Next, arrange five jellied cranberry slices over cake slices. Layer with a third of the pudding mixture, four cake slices, and remaining jellied cranberry. Cover with remaining pudding and top with remaining cake slices. Use your clean hands to press down gently. Cover with plastic wrap and chill in the refrigerator for one to two hours.

4 Just before serving, remove placenta from the refrigerator. Place the serving platter upside down over the top of the dessert-filled bowl. With an adult's help, carefully invert the dessert from the bowl onto the serving platter. Remove plastic wrap and serve immediately.

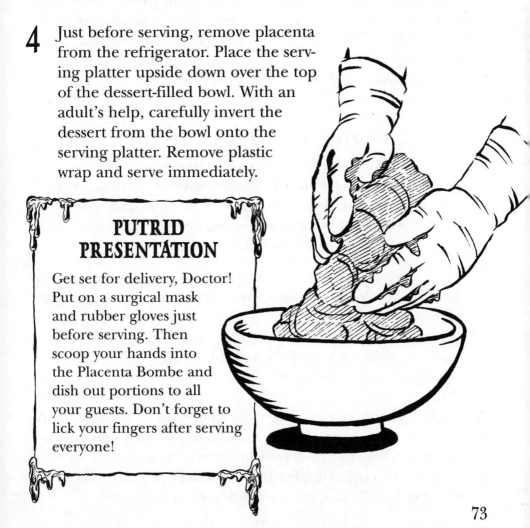

PUTRID PRESENTATION

Get set for delivery, Doctor! Put on a surgical mask and rubber gloves just before serving. Then scoop your hands into the Placenta Bombe and dish out portions to all your guests. Don't forget to lick your fingers after serving everyone!

Pumping-Heart Tart

Here's a dessert they'll eat in a heartbeat!

INGREDIENTS

1 red licorice whip
1 red licorice lace
¾ cup water
1 3-ounce box strawberry gelatin
1 14-ounce can sweetened condensed milk
½ cup sour cream
¼ cup concentrated or fresh lemon juice

1 teaspoon vanilla extract
½ cup plus 1 tablespoon butter or margarine
¼ cup firmly packed brown sugar
1 cup unsifted all-purpose flour
¼ cup quick-cooking oats
¼ cup finely chopped nuts, any type

TOOLS YOU'LL NEED

- 8- to 10-ounce large teacup with a slightly oval interior
- kitchen scissors • no-stick cooking spray • small saucepan
- pot holders • fork • clear tape • medium mixing bowl
- wire whisk • large mixing bowl • electric mixer
- 12-inch round pizza pan, greased

1 With an adult's help, use scissors to cut licorice whip and shoelace licorice in half, as major arteries and smaller tributary veins. Set aside. Spray interior of teacup with no-stick cooking spray.

2 With an adult's help, heat water to boiling in saucepan and remove from heat. Use pot holders to place pan on a heat-safe work surface, then pour in strawberry gelatin. Use a fork to stir until completely dissolved. Pour gelatin into the teacup. Refrigerate the remainder for eating later.

3 Bend a section of licorice shoelace into a "U" shape and place it in the teacup. If necessary, you can use clear tape to keep it propped upward. Refrigerate until firm, about three hours.

4 To make filling, combine sweetened condensed milk, sour cream, lemon juice, and vanilla in a mixing bowl. Mix well with a wire whisk. Cover and chill for at least forty minutes.

5 To make crust, have an adult help you. First, preheat the oven to 350 degrees. Next, in a large mixing bowl, use the electric mixer to combine butter or margarine and brown sugar and beat until fluffy. Add flour, oats, and finely chopped nuts. Mix thoroughly. Press dough into greased pizza pan, bringing dough all the way to edges.

6 With an adult's help, place pizza pan in oven and bake for ten to twelve minutes or until golden brown. Use pot holders to remove and place on a heat-safe work surface.

7 When crust has cooled completely, spread tart filling evenly over crust. Lay remaining licorice shoelace over the center of the tart. Then invert pumping heart onto tart's center, directly over licorice shoelace. (To help loosen heart from mold, gently shake and tap the sides of the teacup.)

8 Push licorice whips through the heart, so they stick out evenly on both sides. Now, your "arteries" will protrude from the upper and lower heart. When serving the tart, give each person a little piece of your heart, too.

Serves: 8 "hearty" eaters

Poached Seagull Droppings

Look! Up in the sky! It's a bird! Not just any bird—it's a giant seagull delivering your fresh dessert. . . . Look out below . . . SPLAT!!!

INGREDIENTS

6 pears

3 tablespoons blackstrap molasses

½ cup very warm water

¾ cup pancake syrup

3 2-inch cinnamon sticks

1 teaspoon vanilla

6 whole cloves

2 cups sour cream

½ cup granulated sugar

TOOLS YOU'LL NEED

- vegetable peeler • 13 by 9 by 2-inch baking dish
- medium mixing bowl • wire whisk • heavy-duty aluminum foil
- pot holders • turkey baster • small mixing bowl
- rubber spatula

1   With an adult's help, preheat oven to 350 degrees. Then have an adult help you carefully peel pears and remove stems. Use your peeler to carefully dig out core and seeds from the bottom of pears.

2   Place pears in 13 by 9 by 2-inch baking dish, stem-side up. Combine molasses, water, pancake syrup, cinnamon sticks, vanilla, and cloves in a medium mixing bowl. Whisk together ingredients to thoroughly blend. Pour mixture over pears. Cover baking pan with heavy-duty foil.

3   With an adult's help, use pot holders to place dish in oven. Bake for ten minutes, then have an adult take the dish out of the oven. Carefully uncover and baste well using your turkey baster. Have adult return baking dish to the oven.

4 Repeat step 3 every ten minutes for a total of forty minutes or until pears are tender. Have adult remove from oven, then allow pears to cool slightly in syrup.

5 Just before serving, place 2 cups sour cream and ½ cup sugar into a small mixing bowl and blend well using a rubber spatula to create a base for the droppings.

6 Plop ½ cup of the sour cream mixture onto the center of each dessert plate by letting it drop off the spatula, from about 8 inches above platter, and onto plate. Place one pear in the center of each turd base. Create a naturally runny, fresh seagull dropping appearance by spooning a few tablespoons of extra sauce from the baking dish over white area of turd. Seagull droppings are great served warm or chilled.

Serves: 6 bird watchers

Dead Roach Torte Surprise

What do you do with a roach-infested kitchen?
Bake those little buggers!

INGREDIENTS

½ cup seedless dates or prunes

1 10-inch round angel food cake

2 3-ounce packages cream cheese

1 14-ounce can sweetened condensed milk

⅓ cup concentrated or fresh lemon juice

1 teaspoon almond extract

1 12-ounce container ready-made whipped topping

1 cup slightly mashed fresh blueberries

TOOLS YOU'LL NEED

• small utility knife • large serrated knife • cake plate
• large mixing bowl • electric mixer • rubber spatula

1 *Serves: 16 hungry fetuses*

To create crawling roaches, remove pits from your dates or prunes. With an adult's help, use utility knife to make three equal-sized cuts into a date or prune (see illustration). Leave the top third uncut. Then carefully fan out the two outside cut portions to create two wings. Finally, peel up two tiny strips of date or prune peel from the uncut portion to form antennae. Repeat this for all the prunes or dates, leaving two completely uncut. Set aside.

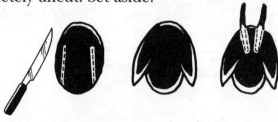

2 To make a cockroach tunnel, cut your ready-made cake in two, widthwise, and hollow out the larger lower portion. Here's how: Ask an adult to use a large serrated knife to cut the angel food cake in two, from side to side, starting about an inch from the top. Set this top portion aside to be used as the cake's lid. Then, to hollow out the lower portion of cake, ask an adult to help you use the serrated knife to cut along the outer rim of cake, about an inch in from the edge. Cut down into the cake

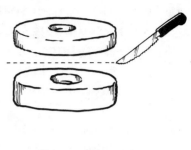

and stop about an inch from the bottom. Carry knife all around outer rim of cake in an up-and-down sawing motion.

3 Next, repeat this same method along the inner rim of the cake. Cut about an inch from the inner rim and an inch from the bottom. Finally, use your clean hands to gently scoop out cake's cut center to form a hollow tube in the center of your cake.

4 Tear removed cake bits from center into bite-sized bits. Set aside.

5 With an adult's help, place cream cheese in large mixing bowl and, with an electric mixer, beat until fluffy. Gradually add sweetened condensed milk, lemon juice, and almond extract. Continue beating until mixture is smooth and well blended.

6 Using the rubber spatula, gently fold in 1 cup ready-made whipped topping (reserve the rest for frosting the cake), dates or prunes, cake pieces, and mashed blueberries. Fill cake's hollowed out portion with this dead roach mixture and carefully replace cake's lid.

7 Finally, use the rubber spatula to frost cake with remaining ready-made whipped topping. Decorate with two crawling uncut roaches. Place cake in freezer and chill for three to four hours before serving.

Serves: 10 to 12 little buggers

PUTRID PRESENTATION

Brush the bottom of a new sneaker with nontoxic poster paint. Then make a footprint on a square of heavy construction paper or poster board. Make one for each guest. When paint has dried, cut out shoe print—treads and all—and use it as a serving platter for your Dead Roach Torte.

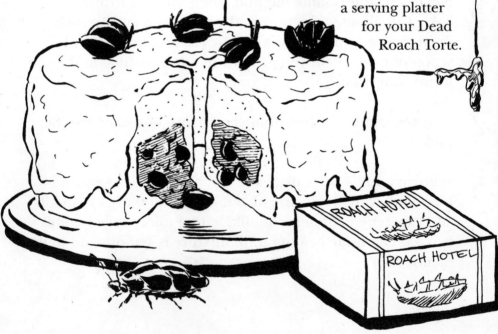